TO
ROBERDA ~~B~~ DE MARCO'S LAW
AND
BILL
   ALWAY REMEMBER DEMARCO'S
LAW. NO MATTER WHAT ALWAYS
RECOVER AND PRESS ON.

      Fred D

DE MARCO'S LAW

LOUIS DE MARCO

Elderberry Press

⩰ Elderberry Press
1393 Old Homestead Drive, Second floor
Oakland, Oregon 97462—9506.
E-MAIL: editor@elderberrypress.com
TEL/FAX: 541.459.6043

All Elderberry books are available from your favorite bookstore, amazon.com, or from or our 24 hour order line: 1.800.431.1579

Publisher's Catalog-in-Publication Data
De Marco's Law/Louis De Marco
ISBN 1-930859-06-6

1. Self-help.
2. Perseverance.
3. Philosophy.
4. Anecdotes.
5. Memoir.
I. Title

This book was printed, and bound in the United States of America

DE MARCO'S LAW

Thank you Dolores Cyr for all your help

"It's not the amount or size of the mistake that counts. What counts is how well you recover.

PRESS ON...

on't Quit

When things go wrong as they some times will;
When the road you're trudging seems all uphill;
When the funds are low, and the debts are
high;
and you want to smile, but have to sigh;

When care is pressing you down a bit—
Rest if you must, but don't quit.
Success is failure turned inside out;
The silver tint of the clouds of doubt;
And you can never tell how close you are;
It may be near when it seems afar.
So stick to the fight when you're hardest hit—
It's when things go wrong that you mustn't
quit.

—Author Unknown—

Say, I can, I can, I can, instead of I can't, I can't I can't. I can't only means I don't want to, or I don't want to think about it. Remember De Marco's Law recover and

PRESS ON…

*L*ife is What YOU Make It

Outside my window a new day I see,
and only I can determine
What kind of day it will be.

It can be busy and sunny, laughing and gay,
or boring and cold, unhappy and gray.

My own state of mind is the determining key,
for I am the only person I let myself be.

I can be thoughtful and do all I can to help,
or be selfish and think just of myself.

I can enjoy what I do and make it seem fun,
or gripe and complain and make it hard on
someone.

I can be patient of those who may not understand,
    or belittle and hurt them as much as I can.

    But I have faith in myself,
    and believe what I say,
    and personally I intend
    to make the best of each day.
    —anonymous—

Remember if you can think it, or dream it, it
can happen. You must find your destiny in yourself.
The past you can't change, the future you can change.

prologue

urphy's Law — If something can go wrong it will go wrong. This is a negative law.

De Marco's Law- Is a positive law and is to correct Murphy's Law.

While in the Air Force one of my very intelligent good friends used to get upset when things didn't go just right.

One day he told me, "you know, Lou, you seem to always recover and move on with life no matter what happens." I thought that was true and developed De Marco's Law soon after this incident.

Most people have no idea of their capabilities and what they can be. We must look at the inside not the outside of not only other people but of ourselves.

When you are down it may be a time to make some changes. You must always be adaptable to making these changes. Don't be one of those people who keeps making the same mistakes over and over. To be a great leader you must see the future first.

Remember it is much better to be a joyologist then a pessimist. Make every day a holiday. You can't feel down in the mouth with the corners turned up.

Always recover and

PRESS ON...

one

THE HAPPY LINE

Many people have a very serious problem staying happy if they ever drop back from their highest point in life. The reason may be finance, fame or many other problems.

To explain the "Happy Line" to other people put out a hand and say, everything above this line you are happy and every thing below this line you are unhappy. The higher above the line the happier you are. The farther you go below the line the more you are unhappy.

The problem so many people have is, they keep raising their "Happy Line". If they had raised their position in such ways as money, fame, physical or in any way that was higher then their present situation, they become unhappy and this unhappiness can become extreme.

There are many examples, such as movies stars, athletes, business people and many other areas. When their fame or finances have declined, even though after the reduction they may still be at a higher level then they had been originally, they now become very unhappy.

In order for these people to become happy again they must lower their "Happy Line". They must look at other people who have so much less then they have in money, looks, fame or what ever they lost and see how happy they are. Look at all the wonderful things that you have had in life. Look at all of the people who have less then you, but are very happy, lower your "Happy Line".

Be positive. I ask my students in college to give me three positive examples of things that had the most effect on their lives. I give them my three examples.

First, I am glad my grandparents sacrificed to come to the United States.

Second, I am glad that I had great caring and loving parents.

Third, I am so glad they did not have birth control in those days.

I was the ninth of eleven children. If they had birth control I would not be here. A sense of humor is always helpful to keep you and others around you in a happy mood. Look to the positive. Remember every day above the ground is a good day. You can be as happy as you make up your mind to be. Don't let people label you. Labels should be on food and clothes not on people.

two

FRIENDLY AS A CAT IN A FISH MARKET

Many people have a problem picking friends. A true or real friend is someone you can call three o'clock in the morning if you have a problem. This true friend will get out of bed, even if they aren't feeling well, and gladly come to your aid. The rest of the people that we usually call good friends are actually special acquaintances. Many of the people we call our friends are like the "Cat in the fish market" that rubs against you and purrs so sweetly to get what it wants. Watch those good weather friends that rush to you when you are in a special position that can help them. That is why many people who become rich or famous keep their old friends.

A special friend can be many types of people.

They can be old classmates, military, business, old neighbors and many other types of friends that now live far away. Our new society forces us to move often, but we should keep our ties to these special friends.

One of the worse combination of friends is if you have a group of three as your best friends. This is a very dangerous combination, because many times two of these friends will get together and leave out the third friend., The third friend who has many times told other people how close you three were can now be devastated.

Remember you can disagree and still be agreeable.

PRESS ON...

three

SHOOK AS A WOODPECKER IN A PETRIFIED FOREST

As long as we live we will make some kind of mistakes. When you visit a cemetery, look at the pictures of those who died, or think about them. Just think they are not lucky enough to be able to make new mistakes.

When you are down, think about others that were down or other times that you were down and how well you and others recovered. Some of these mistakes actually improve your future, Many times the greatest risk is not taking one.

Life is how you look at it. The story of the little boy who was pitching the baseball is a good example. He said, "I am the greatest" as he threw the ball up and swung. He missed, strike one. He said, "I am the greatest". He threw up the ball and missed, strike two. He said, "I am the greatest". He threw up the ball again and said, "I am the greatest", he missed, strike three. He then walked away and said, "I am the greatest pitcher".

De Marco's Law – recover and PRESS ON....

Most of us know the biblical story about the one who hasn't committed sin throw the first stone. This is true of all of us. Many times in our lives we have been as shaken as that woodpecker in the petrified forest. The only way that woodpecker or you can survive is to go on and make that experience a growing part of your life.

There are so many ways you can use De Marco's Law to recover.

The story of the Italian selling a horse is another example: A man asked the Italian, "how much do you want for that horse?" The Italian said, "two-hundred dollars". The man buying the horse said, " that is very cheap". The Italian said, "the horse no look a too good". The man said, "he looks good to me" and bought the horse. When he got the horse home he found out that horse was blind, so he took the horse back to the Italian and said, "you sold me a blind horse". The Italian then said, "I told you he no look a too good".

I have had many people come to me and say, "you always say recover and press on, I had this problem and I thought how would Lou De Marco handle it. Then they tell me how they took care of the problem and that it worked out great. What they did is usually not exactly how I would have solved the problem, but they did an excellent job and recovered. I tell them they did a great job. I do not go into great detail about how I would have solved it. There are many different ways to solve problems.

I have also seen many people do a great job recovering and I'm sure if you think about it, and you should think about it, it may help you in your life.

An example that happened to me is a good point. This couple drove through a stop sign in front of me. I swerved and stopped very close to a serious collision. I was very angry and got out of the car to chew the couple out. Before I could say a word this lady got out of the passenger seat and said to me, "you sure are a great driver, it is amazing how you avoided this accident". My anger was now completely gone and I asked how they were and went on my way, a happy person instead of an upset angry person.

Remember some things are so serious, you can't get serious about them. You must take control when things go wrong, don't give up.

PRESS ON...

four

SHEEP

ollow the leaders even if they take you over the cliff.

We are all followers to some degree and in different times of our lives. The problems occur when we follow the wrong leaders ,or we follow to an extreme, or for too long.

Look at how people see beauty in different cultures and in different eras of history. In the United States' early history the type of clothes, hair styles, weight and many other areas were not only very different but they are now looked at as old fashioned. Today in the modern world there are many more options. But the people who will make money from the fashions will put a lot of pressure on you to follow their ideas of fashion. The people who give you the extreme fashions of today will do everything in their power to get us to follow like a herd of sheep. We must not give into people who will try in every way to have us spend our hard earned money on things that will make them wealthy at our expense.

Are you the type of person that follows some one or a group even if you wouldn't do it if the group hadn't done it? Would you take food from a company party because you saw others taking the food for themselves?

Look at how different cultures see beauty. There are countries that put rings on women's necks to lengthen them. While other societies will lengthen peoples lips to extreme proportions. In our society people will go to surgeons to build up their lips. You must get a clear picture of what the effects of going along with society will cost you in health and finances.

We must always spend more on our love for what is on the inside of a person instead of what is on the outside. A wise man can act like a fool, but a fool can't act like a wise man. Don't follow like sheep. Recover and

PRESS ON....

five

HAPPY AS A BABY BEAVER IN A TOOTHPICK FACTORY

Life can be and should be great if you look at it the right way. If you do this you will be as Happy as that Baby Beaver in a Toothpick Factory.

Think about when you had less and were happy. Remember the saying, "you can't stop twice in the same river". Life is like that river. The terrain maybe mostly the same but it is different water.

Circumstances such as finances, physical, age and many more things can change and will change. There are times that you must not only leave the bad things behind, you must also leave the good things behind and PRESS ON...

In the past most people stayed in the same areas and kept the same friends. If you move often, as most of us do in our modern society, you must make the most of a friendship while it lasts. Many friendships now only exist in memory. When we move we should still keep in contact with those best friends. Even if you can't live by them you can still keep in contact.

Many of us have made more than out share of mistakes in our lives. We must learn from our mistakes, leave them behind, and PRESS ON.....

Many people don't leave things behind; now they become super cautious and instead of De Marco's Law, they go to Paul's Law which says, "you can't fall off the floor".

You do not even have to apologize for every mistake. Many people apologize and continue to make the same mistakes. If you now move in the right direction most people will notice it and appreciate what you are now doing.

If we can't change or improve on some things in life we must use De Marco's Law and make the most of it. There are many examples.

Jimmy Durante used his large nose to make himself rich and famous. Many people look at such things as their extra weight as a gift and use it to their advantage. Remember it is how we look at things not what society says it should be. The little child looks at his parents and grandparents as the greatest. He does not look at their financial or physical side. We must remember how we enjoyed the small things when we had less in life. We must look at our special areas of talent not our weak spots and this includes the physical side.

We must look at the great pleasures in our life and there are so many great pleasures that any misfortune can not take away all those great joys in life. Remember it is your life! You can do it! David beat Goliath because he used other tactics than direct contact. You can always find ways to move on. You must use the word

impossible with great caution. Because you have a difference of opinion does not mean you have a difference in principle. Look at the whole picture. The real valuable things in life are free - family and friends. Remember beauty is in the eyes of the beholder and so is everything else.

six

A MARTHA HOWARD

*T*here are people that must always have everything perfect. I call these people "A Martha" for Martha Stewart. There are also people that fear germs to the extreme, as Howard Hughes did especially in his later years. I call these people "Howard". Many people that have a "Howard" tendency also lean toward perfection. I call these people "Martha Howards".

It can be a very good thing, especially at certain times and in certain situations to be extremely clean, such as hospitals and food areas. It is also important to do things to perfection in many areas, such as surgery. The problems occur when we do a "Martha" or "Howard" in every action of our lives. If we have these problems to extreme and use them at the wrong times we can weaken or destroy friend-ships or our goals in life.

I have seen "Marthas" in action many times in the Air Force. I have had navigator students worry about paper work instead of keeping up with and staying ahead of the aircraft. I have seen new pilots in emergencies worry about small things instead of the real problems. In politics, I have seen the poorly qualified dwell on the little things because they couldn't handle the big problems.

Think about who you are dealing with, what's the situation and when you should use a "Martha" or "Howard". We become what we think about most of the time.

PRESS ON...

seven

YOU CAN'T STEAL SECOND

You Can't Steal Second With Your Foot On First

Clear your mind of can't.

Remember it's not the load that will break you down, it's the way you carry that load. There are millions of people that had very little and moved themselves into very high positions. Coach Knute Rockne is a very good example. He revolutionized the game of football by focusing constantly on improvement.

As a 19-year-old dispatcher, Knute Rockne was trying to come up with a way to get ahead. Then it hit him! Look for better ways to do things, better than anyone else.

After saving enough for college, he headed straight for Notre Dame. Rockne was persistent. His initial football attempt was a scratch, so in his sophomore year he decided to throw his efforts into track. With a winning record there, Rockne gave football another shot. Finally, he made third string in his junior year.

That wasn't good enough for Rockne. To get ahead, he spent nearly every free minute he had during the summer before senior year practicing football passes with a friend.

He analyzed his weak spots. Rockne figured out that he was more likely to fumble when the ball bounced against his arms and chest. So he began catching the ball with his fingers, like a baseball player. His new technique helped the team beat archenemy Army in 1913. We must remember to never stop learning. We must continue training and acquire skills. It's not the load that breaks you down, it's the way you carry it.

De Marco's Law believes how you think is everything. Remember it is a positive law. You must always think positive, beware of a negative environment and work hard. Success is a marathon, not a sprint. Never give up. Don't be afraid to innovate and be different. Following the herd can take you over a cliff.

Rockne tried to keep an eye on the long term. He wanted to know what his team might look like come fall, so he developed spring practice, now common at most schools.

Long after the players had left Notre Dame the players continued to come to him with their problems. He continued to give comfort and advise to all who sought it.

Another good example is railroad developer, James Hill, born in a log cabin, Hill was 14 when his father died. He had to leave school after just nine years and go to work to support his family.

When Hill talked about building a railroad from Chicago to the west coast and up into Canada, critics scoffed at him. Not only couldn't he build a money making transcontinental railroad, but he was going to do it without government hand outs. Hill held tightly to his vision. As a result, while all other transcontinental railroads of the late 19th century sought shelter under bankruptcy and government help, Hill prospered because he was a keen watcher of the way business and the economy worked.

Most transcontinental railways relied on federal money. Hill shunned federal aid. He feared such help would lead to political control of his railroads. To be successful you must have self-confidence, but you must also always be prepared. Remember you are what you believe.

Hill was <u>fully</u> involved in the building of the railroad. He analyzed curves and grades himself. He rode his private car over every inch of track, noting each dip and grade that could be smoothed.

In contrast, the government backed transcontinental became infamous for laying track so it would wind around curves on purpose making the longest possible routes.

Federal aid was based on track miles, so leaders of those railroads built to pile up government payments. They built quickly to meet subsidy deadlines, resulting in badly built and poorly surveyed lines. Remember many professional people will use these tactics to get more money from you.

eight

WHERE I'M COMING

here I'm Coming – Where I'm Going Nobody Knows

The winds will continue blowing and the rivers will still flow

Everybody will continue to be challenged as long as they live. They must be like the wind and the river and keep moving. Always remember De Marco's Law "Recover and Press On". You can't be unhappy if you are doing what you want to do. When you see a group laughing you want to move toward that group. Stay away from the continuous complainers. They can make you believe you can't succeed. We must make a sincere effort to learn much more about what we already know. Always be an optimist. A pessimist will make a small hill a giant mountain while a optimist sees a mountain as a wonderful challenge. Stop saying what you can't do, say what you can do.

Don't let people rule your life. Life is all how you see it, in the monster show. The pretty girl was thought of as the ugly one in the group and the others painted themselves as the good looking group. That is great for the monster group, but it usually isn't good for the person who is cut down. You must rise above it or use De Marco's Law and turn it into an advantage.

You don't have to always be the best person in the world to get ahead, but you must use every opportunity to move forward.. If you are born in royalty you can be the leader of a country. Are you really the best person for the position?

If the laws and society say you are then you can be that person. This isn't only true in royalty it is also true in a democracy. Do you think all the people elected to office at all levels are the best person for that position? They are usually in that position because they were in the right place at the right time. Very often the "golden rule" says those who have the gold make the rules.

In your own life as you are trying to succeed,

remember what Napoleon said, "never interrupt your enemy when he is destroying himself." There are always many people trying to build themselves up, but at your expense. An example is the man who told the women on their first date, "I'm as strong as a horse." The women said, "I don't know if it's true, I've never been out with a horse."

When things aren't going just right you must say my face may be blooded, but my head will not be bowed and remember never take a sleeping pill and a laxative at the same time.

PRESS ON...

nine

HARD TIMES

Recover and PRESS ON...

We will always have a certain amount of hard times in out life. The important thing is we must not only recover and press on but we must actually learn from these hard times and make our lives and the love ones around us lives better. You will not get ahead in life by obsessing on victim hood.

Many people believe they need to know every thing about a subject to succeed and enjoy life. You do not need to know all the ingredients in a pie or any other food to enjoy it. This is also very true about life.

When we move forward in life, we must keep many of the things that we loved when we had less. These items even if they are only pictures can be a great help by putting love in your heart. We never have too much love.

We must not only look at our own lives but we must look at history and people in history who inspired so many people. During Great Britain's worst times during World War II, Churchill promised his people only blood, sweat and tears. Ben Franklin said, "when you are good to others you are good to yourself". Tom Jefferson said, "your dreams of the future are made better when you know the history of the past". We must always look at our past as a way to learn and move ahead. When Lou Gehrig found out he had a terminal illness said, "I'm the luckiest man on the face of the earth". He was looking at the great things in his life. Isn't that the way we should all look at life?

We all have different likes and dislikes, and should look at our lives and what we enjoy not what others say or their life styles. Life is like the clouds in the sky, it is only there temporarily. We must enjoy it. Remember you can't be a failure if you have friends. Life is too short to hold grudges. After every problem in life we must walk away smarter. We must continue to say I'm a lucky person. Be an optimist not a pessimist. What you give out is what you get back. This also includes your attitude. Life is like a house - what it looks like is not important, what is important is what goes on inside.

You must listen and learn, but you must control your own life. If you listen to T.V. and the movies they can make some people believe that water runs uphill and the sun rises in the west, if they tell you enough times and in many different ways. If a lie gets a head start it is hard to stop. If you repeat a lie hundreds of times and in hundreds of ways it is still a lie.

Yogi Berra said, "when you come to a fork in the road take it". This is so true, when you take that fork in the road always make the most of it, and if for some reason it is the wrong road or it's time to change direction, first study the facts and then recover and press on. It is never too late to be what you might have been

You must seize and enjoy every minute of life. Look at it and really see it, live it. Recover and PRESS ON....

ten

ON THE OTHER HAND

A one arm person can not say, "on the other hand"

We continuously hear people say that they were left out some how in life and that is why they are having all of these problems

It is not resources that limit economic growth and life styles, but human ingenuity. Two centuries ago, Thomas Malthus declared that world wide famine was inevitable as human population growth out paced food production. In 1972 a group of scholars known as the Club of Rome predicted much the same thing for the waning years of the 20th century. It didn't happen because human ingenuity has out paced population growth. There are many countries in Europe where the population would actually decline if it were not for immigration.

You can't find the truth with both eyes closed. Always look up rather then down. To win you must be on the offense. The weak do not inherit the earth. Very often we must co-op other people's ideas.

Your future can't be written. It is only what you make it. You can clone a person, but that person will not be the same person. The clones may look a like but they will be completely different individuals. What they will become will depend on many factors. They will not necessarily be even the same height or weight. It depends on many things such as food, exercise and mental areas.

Our fallibility's can actually be a positive in life if you remember De Marco's Law. Recover and PRESS ON.... Our founding Fathers had many fallibility's, but in spite of these fallibility's they actually helped to make our country great.

Life is like an itch that won't go away with one scratch. You must keep improving your life. If farmers don't plow and plant seeds they will be in shock when fall comes and there isn't any crop. You must know what your ideas and actions will bring. If you pay five dollars for a paddle that cost six dollars for the manufacturer to make, the manufacturer will soon find that they are up the creek without a paddle. You must not play the under dog role. It will only keep you down.

Rich shouldn't be how much money you have.. Rich is how you look at life. A good example is the person who had twins, one was an optimist and the other one was a pessimist. The father took them to a psychologist. The psychologist tried an experiment. He said, "we will put the pessimist in a room filled with toys and the optimist is a room filled with manure." They later went by the room with the pessimist and he was crying. When asked why he was crying, he said, "if I play with these toys I might break them." They then went to the room full of manure. The optimist was laughing and throwing manure around the room. The optimist said, " with all this manure there is bound to be a pony here some where."

When Ronald Reagan became president the United States was in a deep recession. The Soviet Union was our arch enemy and the country was wailing in pessimism. Reagan had a lot to do with not only getting us out of the recession, but as he predicted the evil empire is no more. A great leader must be an optimist.

Every revolution starts with one person, why can't that one person be you? You must know when to take chances and how to work with others. Lewis and Clark took many chances and found ways to work together as a team. They had a common purpose. Their adventure helped to make it possible for our great president Thomas Jefferson, who sent them on this mission, to bring this area into the union.

Leaders must know how to follow and must pick strong and competent people. There are actually many leaders that do not want competent people under them because they are afraid they will take their position. These people end as failures. You must rely on your confidence not your doubts. There are also times when leaders need to show humility. There are also times when you should show indifference to what others say you should do or can do. This can be the right decision if you know what you are doing. You do not always need to learn all the ways to be an expert by being taught by an expert. You often need to learn by experience. Some people need to keep looking for their direction in life. Remember you can't win unless you run. Don't just want success, expect you can do it. It's not the size of the dog but how hard it bits.

You must learn how to think not what to think. You should always have a good compass and be a good navigator. Put your gear up this will speed up results. Anybody can cheer when they win, it takes a special person to get up and go when you are down. Don't abandon the lady you took to the dance. Remember Yogi Berra. It's not over till it's over. Lets hope the mountains we have to climb are always small. There is always a light at the end of the tunnel, but there will always be other tunnels, you must use your experiences to handle this tunnel better then past ones and even enjoy many of the challenges.

Remember De Marco's Law   Recover and PRESS ON....

eleven

THE KNIFE

Would you rather be cleaning the knife in the kitchen or using the knife in surgery?

Ben Franklin said, "even the sun has spots, warts and all". We all have problems and short comings. Look at some of the people you know personally and famous people. If you really had to judge many of these people before they made their mark in life, would you pick all of them as winners in their area? Look at Yogi Berra. Did he really look like a hall of fame baseball player? Yogi not only became a great ball player, he used what we call short comings to be a famous person in other ways. You can't be good at something unless you think you can be good at it.

Many times we must fight fire with fire. We can develop way beyond what we or others think is possible. Remember the rich man gets ice in the summer, the poor man gets ice in the winter. Think enough of yourself to be yourself. The hardest work on the planet is thinking, thinking isn't dangerous not thinking is. The greatest gift you can give anyone is teaching them to think for themselves.

PRESS ON....

twelve

EXERCISE THE MIND AND BODY

Use it or Lose it
Brain power like muscle power that isn't used is lost. You must love yourself and your body, as you age. You must continue to try to improve yourself. A proper diet and exercise can ward off most diseases. How you look is not what you were born with but how you package it. If you take crap and paint it you just have painted crap. You must add life to your years, as you add years to your life, always remembering it's not your age but your attitude.

Don't be the person that is always saying I wish I could, I should have done it this way or that way. Nothing can really stop you but you. Don't put your life on cruise control. Think about consequences, don't be like the lady who stopped taking estrogen in the winter so that she would have hot flashes and save on her heating bill.

You must exercise all of your body not just parts of it. Remember the best sex organ is between the ears not the legs.

Men and women are from earth not Mars or Venus. How your life turns out depends on how you live and see your life. Behavior will create the hormones that send your mind and body in the right or wrong direction. Don't just know how to count but what counts. People with mental problems often whine about all the things they see as problems in their lives. Don't complain about every little thing, what's more important are the sum total of your experiences.

Look at all the facts before you come to a conclusion. You must look at the small facts to put large things together. The placebo effect is a good example of how the body and mind can be controlled. There is the mere idea of our hope that we can improve or get better that has a large effect on the outcome. In some cases the placebo effect works by stimulating the endorphin system. There are studies that show when people believed that red pills were uppers and blue pills were downers people would respond accordingly.

The saying goes an ounce of prevention is worth a pound of cure, and it may even save you money.

According to a study people age 65 and over saved an average of $196 per month in health cost, such as doctors, hospitalization and medicine.

There are many kinds and ways to exercise. Depending on your situation. You must first check out what type of exercise is best for you in your present situation. This could be your present health, climate, financial and many other areas.

If you expect to continue exercising you must enjoy it. It is very important for most people if they think of it as recreation and fun first and for your health second. You can make all exercise fun if you just start out at a very low level and continue to improve. Companionship is another very important factor.

You don't have to join a gym, but gyms can be excellent. What if a gym isn't available or unaffordable? Go for walks, ride a bike, take jazzercise, but make it enjoyable. You don't appreciate what you have until you don't have it – including your health.

So you have let your health deteriorate, remember De Marco's Law. It's not the amount or

size of the mistake that counts, what counts is how
well you recover
       PRESS ON...

thirteen

PAUL'S LAW

*Y*ou can't fall off the floor

There are times in all our lives when we should be very cautious, but we can't use Paul's Law to the extreme. There are people who are so cautious that they actually don't want to leave their home or be around other people because they are afraid they will do or say something wrong.

There are also people who go to the opposite extreme and take wild chances that can destroy their fortunes or even their lives. Many of the people who go bankrupt (and some do it more than once) do not look at the whole picture. They are so excited about making the big money. Those that fail the first time should look at De Marco's Law and find out what went wrong and now either drop the idea, go in a different direction, or improve on your idea, but don't give up on life. Remember anybody who never made a mistake in life, never made a discovery.

PRESS ON...

fourteen

BIRDS OF A FEATHER
FLOCK TOGETHER

*I*n behavior psychology you must look at the source of your information. People usually pick an occupation or organization that goes along with their beliefs.

Lets look at some occupations that feed us so much information. Most of the people who are in the professions such as movies, print and television are on the left side of the spectrum. Those in business will tend to the right. The media has a lot of power over the control of your thoughts. Remember they don't have to pay to put out propaganda. They will continue to hit a subject in a certain way until they can get you to think their way. Do you ever notice how they will stick things in movies, TV and other areas of communication to influence your position? They usually do it in a very sly way where you don't know they are doing it. They will continue to repeat or laugh at something until they get you to go their way. A good example is ketchup as a vegetable. Remember how they continued to laugh about ketchup as a vegetable in the school lunch program. Many people love ketchup and they will load it on many foods. Another condiment that has become even more popular then ketchup is salsa.

Let's look at what is in ketchup. Ketchup has a very important ingredient for your health called lycopene.

Lycopene is an antioxidant that shows promise as a cancer and heart disease prevention agent.

The reason lycopene is higher in ketchup is that when processed lycopene in tomatoes is converted and changed into something more readily absorbed by the body.

Heinz institute research reveals that not only is lycopene stored in the liver, lungs., prostrate gland, colon and skin, but studies also suggest that lycopene may restrain the growth of prostrate, digestive tract, breast, lung and cervical cancer. Added to this list are inhibitions in the development of cardiovascular disease and age related muscular degeneration.

Why don't we hear more about this study?

In life we must always look at the source of our information. Your perception of positive or negative is somewhere behind the eyes. Be positive and don't believe everything you hear or read no matter how many times you hear it or read about it.

PRESS ON...

fifteen

STRESS

*Y*ou must learn how to handle stress

You must be one of the people that actually like a certain amount of stress. Some athletes, business people, military and many others actually enjoy some of the stress that goes on in life. Triggered by stress, your built-in-flight can save your life in times of danger. If you have the right response to stress it will enhance your mental activity, quicken your response time and give you that very important edge you need to perform your best in challenging situation. The problem many people have is they don't use De Marco's Law and recover instead they continuously increase their stress. Continuous exposure to stress in a negative way can weaken your body and lead to mental and physical health problems.

In the mental area we usually think of stress as a cause for nervous and many other psychological problems. There have been studies that show stress can make you forgetful. These studies show that chronic exposure to stress hormones accelerates degenerative changes in the brain that lead to memory loss.

Many of us have heard of or seen people we know have a heart attack that was triggered by stress. Stress hormones increase the speed and strength of the heart's pumping action and cause blood vessels to constrict, setting the stage for dangerous rhythm disturbances. They also enhance the clotting potential of the blood, increasing the likely hood of artery clogging blockages that can lead to heart attacks.

There is plenty evidence to support the notion that stress can influence the progression of cancer. Several studies have shown that emotional support not only enhances the well being of cancer patients, it also prolongs their lives. Haven't we all heard about the person who just gave up and died.

When you see a person that loses or gains a lot of weight in a short period of time, there is a good chance this person is under a lot of stress. The stress can be from many factors. Very often it is marriage or financial. People who overeat in response to stress tend to deposit fat in their mid-section, an important predictor of heart disease and diabetes.

Exercise is one of the most effective ways to relieve stress. Physical activity puts a damper on insulin levels, lowers blood pressure and slows the heart rate. It is a great help in reducing or keeping your weight level down and improving your appearance. It can also be a great way to meet people and have a very enjoyable time. Make exercise an enjoyable experience. Learning to deal with everyday happenings in your life will not only improve your life, it may save your life.

When people attack you there are times when the best tactic is to just laugh it off or even make it a positive experience. There are people who love to be on the worst dressed list.

Forgive – Let go and your blood vessels will relax. continuous stress doesn't give the body time to be repaired.

Get Control – It's not what you have but how you see it. Beauty is in the eyes of the be holder and so is everything else. Don't let crap bother you, it will pass. After a storm birds sing, so should you. Paradise is a place in the heart. Obstacles are only obstacles if you think of them as obstacles, remember it is some times better to learn then to win. Let bygones be bygones.

Humor is another way to cope with stress. You must have humor at the top and the bottom of your day. I love to say it's been a great life. Look at all the previous hurdles you have crossed. In many ways haven't they made you a stronger and better person? You must not under estimate what your life has to offer. We must let the past be the past. We must come back from all wars. You must fight to forgive and look forward.

You must be the author of your own life. You must like yourself and believe in what you can do. You are second class only if you think like one, reason like one or perform like one. You don't have to be looking from the outside of the window you can move inside. Many times we must play the hand we are dealt. There are many times when we must turn a problem into a challenge. If you can see it as a challenge it can actually turn out as a positive event. Hope is much sweeter than despair. It is much better to choose to remember the happy times in out past. Don't let the chicken littles who say, "the sky is falling" take over your life. You must be the kind of person who makes happiness contagious not sadness. You must leave many things at the door, and have a positive way of looking at each situation.

You can be a very short person in stature but you can see above the tallest person. Sonny Bono is one of many examples. Look at how he moved ahead not only as an entertainer but he became a very respected congressman. Desi Arnez came to the USA with a guitar and fifteen cents. We are all imperfect people and we will be judged by imperfect people. Failure is not an option we must live every day with peace and hope. There are only two kinds of worry, things you can do something about, and things you can't do anything about. You must know the difference. There are many times if you don't know, it is okay to say, "I do not know." If you are following the majority, chances are that you're making lots of mistakes. Common sense fools us most of the time. Very often we see things not as they are, but as we are.

Stop worrying about all the small things, invite friends over even if the carpet wasn't vacuumed or the furniture dusted

Look at all these factors and many more. You can beat stress and actually make it a positive force in your life. Remember De Marco's Law recover and

PRESS ON...

sixteen

THE THRILL SEEKERS

*T*he usual story you hear about "The Thrill Seeker" is that he has a gene that gives him a thirst for thrills and to take chances. They say that "Thrill Seekers" have a high dopamine level.

Should we disqualify people from the military or other positions because they do or don't have a high dopamine level?

There are many reason people want to take chances. Many want a more exciting life. They may want to prove to others that they are fearless and important. That is why they go out of their way to show other people that they can do these dangerous things. Many of these people have a low self esteem and by doing these things they can be part of the group.

On the other hand some have a high self esteem and they seek their thrills for many different reasons. In behavior psychology you can change by changing your environment. When I went into aviation cadets we were one kind of person but after the training we graduated as a very different kind of person. This is true in many ways. The police academy, athletic teams, there are so many ways they can change us.

After training they can perform in a smooth and confident manner. There are many ways to get thrills. You can enjoy the natural "high" or an original idea, and become a minority of one. You must be able to understand the difference between want and need.

PRESS ON...

seventeen

ALCOHOL AND FOOD

Behavioral Problems not a Disease

We teach our brain to crave things, such as alcohol or certain kinds of foods, even certain kinds of foods during certain seasons, holidays, time of day, color, texture or even it's name. Many times companies and restaurants will give a food or dish a special name so that you will desire it.

The same is true with alcohol and many other items. Many people will eat or drink certain things because they believe it is the thing to do, and that we must drink certain things on certain occasions.

This can be not only good, but it can be very enjoyable if it is done for the right reasons and in the right amount.

We will often drink or put other things in our body to be part of the crowd, to be the center of attention or at least part of the group. This is done very often and can be good if it is done in the right way and in moderation.

Many times drinking is a phase in our lives or a ritual. It can be during college days, in groups such as sport teams and clubs. If we don't get into serious trouble during this phase it can just be a learning part of our lives. Remember drinking or drugs are not just what college kids are suppose to do.

Do you have other things to do to make you part of the crowd or other things in life that are more important and fulfilling? If not, you should direct your life away from the need for these substitutes such as alcohol, drugs and food, into other areas. You must do this before it gets out of control.

There are those that say it is a gene risk, but when you look at this you will see it isn't true. When you look at your life or other people's lives, don't you see people trying to mold their lives, traditions and values after other people? We may think it is the thing to do even if it is wrong for us. It becomes a self fulfilling prophecy.

Many people believe that when they get high they will have more fun. This isn't so, they can do the same thing if they were alcohol or drug free. They must look at what they plan to do before they do it. They should ask is it really fun or am I being stupid, making a fool of myself, or putting myself and others into dangerous situations. Then they must evaluate and change their attitude about life.

Those with low self esteem who think they need to be part of the crowd by over indulging can do it all without alcohol or drugs and still have self control. I have seen people hypnotized and then given a glass of water and told it was alcohol. Even though there was no alcohol in the drink they acted drunk just by believing it was alcohol.

Our country is different from some other countries in how it treats alcohol problems. We seem to depend mainly on AA. Though AA is successful sometimes, and a good program, the amount of people that go through AA and stay cured is a small percentage of the people with alcohol problems.

There are many more people that you don't hear about or you didn't even notice had a problem with alcohol have now corrected their serious drinking problem and may even still drink, but now in moderation. They have learned proper drinking and responsible drinking. They do not have anymore need to over indulge. Does a person who is one hundred pounds overweight have to stop eating? Many of the same things with over indulgence of alcohol are also true with an over indulgence of food.

There are many people who have made a lot of money by putting out diet books. Many times these diets are harmful to your life.

1)	The diet may have you lose too much weight too fast.

2)	The diet may not provide all the nutrients your body and mind require.

3)	They do not allow you to enjoy those special days, such as holidays when you	can eat other things in moderation.

4)	They are too strict.

5)	They may go into extreme solutions, such as not allowing you to chew food by wiring your mouth so that you can only take in liquids.

6)	When you lose too much weight too fast by giving up too much and too many of the things you enjoy. Very often you will not only go off your diet, but you will indulge to an extreme fashion and gain not only all the weight you lost, but actually put on many more pounds.

It is much better if you lose your weight gradually. I recommend two pounds a month. People have said to me I can lose more than that. Maybe so, but your chances of keeping it off will go way down.

Two pounds a month is twenty four pounds a year. Do not weigh yourself every day, once a week is enough. Be sure you weigh on the same accurate scale and that you do it the same time of day and under the same conditions.

The first pounds are the easiest to lose. As your weight comes down you may have to cut back a little more. After you have lost your weight within ten pounds of your goal, slow the goal down even more. This should set your eating patterns for the rest of your life.

I recommend you cut your fat content. You can do such simple things as going from whole milk to two percent, then one percent, then skim milk. Cut out such things as butter and mayonnaise. You can substitute other items such as salsa. Eat fruit, substitute a banana for peanut M & Ms, reduce the cream in your coffee. Don't super size your food. We often do this to save money. If you super size it, take part of it home. Crunch on carrots instead of high fat foods like potato chips. Eat more baked or broiled instead of breaded and fried. Cut back on fried eggs, meat and toast.

Choose steamed white rice instead of fried rice. Make every meal a feast but without all the heavy fat and calories.

eighteen

CHILDREN

Beauty is in the eyes of the beholder and so is everything else.

In a child's eyes love always means beauty. If you ask a child are your parents or grand-parents beautiful, the answer is a resounding, yes. They also think their parents and grand-parents are the smartest and greatest people in the world. As they grow older they start to see beauty not as a person, but how the media and traditions in their area of the world portrays beauty. When that person gets into the grand-parent age most of them will again see beauty more like they did as a child, wouldn't it be much better if we all continuously saw beauty as the inside of the person the same way children see people?

Children see us as we portray ourselves to them. We had two wonderful children who lived next door to us at our last home. They liked to spend time at out home and they particularly wanted me to play games with them. I told them that my wife was my mother, so they called me Louie and my wife who is younger than me, they called my mother. They would often stop and sit with us when we ate lunch on the porch. One day as my wife went back to the kitchen, I took some food from her plate. They immediately cried out, "your son, your son stole food from your plate.

I believe all children are wonderful. No child is born bad. They do well or poorly in behavior and academics in school depending on their home life and the school atmosphere. You can have identical twins, but one of these children could have had a bad experience that affected their outlook on life. That twin may now do better or worse then the other twin depending on how they looked at the experience.

We have had the GI bill since the end of WWII. The GI bill has had a fantastic affect on the United States economy. The government gives military and former military people a certain amount of money. They can now go to a school of their choice. Why can't poor children's parents have the right to take their children out of a failing school? If they had this choice competition would help make that poor school a much better school.. They could recover and produce a better life.

Teachers must never let children think they can't improve. We do not need ware house schools, where children are labeled and then put in different groups. When you put a person in special education classes they are now labeled for the rest of their lives. These children and all people can move up if they believe they can and are allowed equal opportunity. The best golfers, boxers, drivers and every other group show others how to improve. Why not have the best students show the other students how to improve their grades? After my college students completed the first exam I would then spend a few hours before each new test in group study periods. Each group would have a leader and assistant leader. These leaders were picked by their grades, but this was not mentioned to the students. I would now supervise these study groups, and be sure all of the students participate. The next test grades would take off like a rocket. They were now learning how to study and take tests by the best students. Not only students but all of us have the power of a crouching tiger. We can spring into life, We must never let people track us as bright or dumb, we must always have the belief that we can move up in life.

Love and friendship are extremely important

at all ages, but especially for children. In life we must not total the score on who did the most, especially for your children. When we think back will we ever be able to have the types of friends we had as children? We must spend quality time with our children. Children are children for only so many years. They are like a statue made of snow, it isn't there forever. You can extend it's time but it must disappear as a statue. Childhood can only be kept in pictures and your mind. Think about the question, would you rather live as a king or servant to your children? Many people spend to much time trying to make money instead of enjoying their family. Maybe that is one of the reasons poor kids very seldom commit suicide.

There are many good examples of De Marco's Law at all ages. When the little 5th grade girl was called "four eyes" because she now had to wear eye glasses, she pointed out that Miss Crowder, the prettiest teacher in school, wore eye glasses. She even went a step further: the next time she got teased, she accused her tormentors of being jealous. Her bravado paid off and the kids began to believe her. Some even begged to try on her glasses. Always remember De Marco's Law Recover and

PRESS ON...

They say some children are like waiters they wait for your death. This is only true if you did not give them quality time. There is no life until you've loved and been loved, then there is no death. Enjoy every minute of your children's life, if you've made mistakes in raising your children as we all have, it is time to recover and

PRESS ON...

nineteen

BEING YOUNG TODAY

Jade Cognetti is a very bright and great Young lady. She did this paper and gave me a lot of input on young people today. Here she writes:

If we were all free to act and dress as our own selves with out being pressured by brand names, popularity, and style – wouldn't we all be happier?

Many middle schoolers feel as though there is lots of pressure to wear brand names that are in style to be popular.

**In my interview-roughly, about half of the 13-year-olds I interviewed say they feel pressured to wear brand names, and say they feel more popular wearing the brand named clothes.

Some people will do anything to be popular and be in the "in" crowd. These people are labeled as the "wanna-be's". They try to mold themselves into the kind of people that are in a certain group they want to be in. These people seem to basically lose their own unique identity and become a walking, talking, model of someone else.

Other "wanna-be's" will first try to endear themselves towards popular people, sometimes subconsciously. Even if the popular people aren't true people you would really want to become friends with , some people admit to trying to become friends with them for awhile just because it makes them feel more popular.

**1 out of 3 people say they've acted friendly towards people they usually wouldn't like, just because they're popular.

Sometimes, people have other ways of becoming popular. They don't need to wear brand names or be in style, they just pick on other people. This makes that person gain power and feel better than everyone else. If someone puts you down, all the power you lost was put into them.

Most of the time, people wonder why popular people are even popular. Students say that they view the "preps" as being the most popular. While many of the "wanns-be's" try to be accepted into this group.

**2 out of 3 people say they hate popular people and don't see what the big deal is.

Do you see some of the same things we went through when we were young. The big difference for the grand-parents is that most of us were poor and we couldn't afford expensive clothes, and we didn't even know what brand named clothes were. Isn't it a shame that people that are so poor and maybe on welfare think they need brand named clothes. Young people today must understand how important education is. You can not push the ocean back with a spoon. You need education. Anything that is worth while is not easy.

twenty

SENIOR CITIZENS

A friend gave me this "Stay Young" many years ago, but I can't remember who gave it to me

Stay Young

Youth is not a time of life. Nobody grows old by merely living a number of years. People grow old by deserting their ideas. Years may wrinkle the skin, but to give up enthusiasm wrinkles the soul. Worry, doubt, self-distrust, fear and despair, these are the long, long years that bow the head, and turn your spirit to dust. Whether eighty or fourteen there is in every heart, the sweet amazement at the undaunted challenge, events and joy that your life a head has to give you. You are as young as yourself-confidence, as old as your doubts, as young as the faith in your-self, as old as your fears. So long as your heart re-ceives messages of beauty, courage and cheer.

That is how long you are young. Spend your days thinking about the wonderful times in your life. Think about how lucky you are. Put a big smile in your heart. As you slide down the banister of life may the splinters never point the wrong way, and may you be buried in a coffin of a hundred year oak whose seed you will plant tomorrow. Always remem-ber it is better to be on the right side of the grass, and that humor is like a feather pillow..... It is filled with what is easy to get but gives great comfort. We must not fear old age, we must continue to contrib-ute to society.

Every minute that moves on your clock is an unrepeatable miracles. We can use it, or waste it. Time doesn't pass we do. We must think of retire-ment as an advancement, you are now moving to another life style. Remember De Marco's Law-re-cover and

PRESS ON...

twenty-one

YOU CAN BEAT THE SYSTEM

We must continue to look at behavior patterns

Very often we complain about the crowds, how we had to wait in long lines, or by the time you got there, everything was gone. I believe it is much better to look at behavior to recover and PRESS ON....

There are many examples. If you arrive at an amusement park at opening time, do not go to the first attraction. Look at the park program to see where the attractions are located, then walk very fast deep into the park to your favorite location. If that line is too long immediately go to your second choice.

When you go to a buffet dinner if the line to the meat area is presently too long skip that area and go to other areas and get the other food. that you desire. It is best to check all the food before you put them on your plate as they normally put the cheapest food at the start of the line so that you will fill your plate before you get to the more expensive items. You can now go get a good seat, enjoy the food on your plate and as the line gets shorter now go get that food.

Another good example is a child's Easter egg hunt. Tell the children to skip the first items, get ahead of the other children and then start picking up the eggs. I would train my children before we went to the event and they did just great. It is best to teach children behavior patterns when they are young. It teaches them how to think and plan ahead. They will need this to be a leader.

There are so many ways to use behavior to beat the system and be successful. If we fail today remember De Marco's law recover and

PRESS ON...

twenty-two

THE U.S.A.

When an American thinks about their country, the first thing they should think about is George Washington the father of their country. He might have been king, but refused any such notion. He made that clear in his refusal to run for president for a third term. During the revolutionary war he fought nine battles but only won three battles. Getting knocked down isn't the biggest problem, not getting up is the biggest problem. In out lives we must always remember if we lose something today there will always be another day. In war as in life the winner is the one who wins the last battle. Learn from the loses, remember De Marco's law recover and PRESS ON....

In the lower grades we were taught that George Washington never told a lie in the story about who cut down the cherry tree. We were also told many other stories including the one about throwing a coin across the river. These stories served as a lesson to us whether they were actually true or not. We learned that we must not tell lie's and always try to be a good person and a great leader. The stories about George Washington have remained with us as we honor him through out the USA.

The USA is not made up of one nationality or religion . We are from every kind of back ground and as the years go by the nationalities and religions continue to change, but the American people think of the USA as one country. I don't know of any other country that says a Pledge of Allegiance to it's flag. (We not only stand during the Pledge, we also place our right arm toward the flag, but this was changed after the nazi salute.) Americans also stand and are very proud of their National Anthem.

<u>We must always remember our Veterans</u> This is part of a speech I gave as mayor on Memorial Day.

I have always spent Memorial Day in the audience listening to the speakers, but my mind always wandered off to my flight members who gave their lives so that not only we Americans can live in freedom, but they were also sacrificing for millions of people freedoms in other countries. When I go to my military reunions,

I see my flight mates as they grow old, but I can only picture my departed friends as young men. These men's sacrifices did not only affect their lives but also the lives of their loved ones. The parents whose love of their child means more than their own lives. The spouses who lost their best friend and companion for life. The children who didn't get the pleasure of their dad holding their hand going for walks, watching them in their activities as they grow up, not getting the great pleasure of dad telling them what it was like when he was their age. When I think of these things I start to choke up so I must direct my thoughts to other areas.

On Memorial Day when we think about all those who gave their lives for our freedom we should include Nathan Hale a 21 year old patriot who said, "I only regret that I have only one life to give for my country," but wouldn't it be better if he didn't have to give his life for our freedom? Wouldn't it be better if people would not have to sacrifice their precious lives for our freedom?

Today as we remember all those who gave the ultimate sacrifice for our freedom, we can be grateful that we are at peace.

Our mission and our message is simple; we must not waste the sacrifice of the men and women who bought that freedom with their lives.

Today many schools and colleges do not allow military recruiters in their schools. This is a slap in the face to all of those that sacrificed for their country. There are many wars that some people think we would have been better off if we had not got involved. On this list they may include the Spanish American War, World War I, and Vietnam. We must obey the laws of the land, whether it is the speed limit, military or another legal law.

Lets make all Memorial Days be about those who sacrificed in the past not the present. Always remember they gave their tomorrow for our today. After every war we must recover and

PRESS ON...

twenty-three

IF

*I*f a frog had wings it wouldn't hit it's butt every time it hopped.

If my family had more money. If I were taller. If I were thinner. If I were a man. If I were a woman. If I were of a different race. If I were of a different nationality.

IF—IF—IF

Well you aren't, and that frog doesn't have wings, and bumping its butt is the least thing it has to worry about. Instead of "IFing" you should look at all of those people that have not only prevailed with your so called problems, but have moved on to a very happy life. Every time you point out what you call a short fall or a problem it doesn't help you. What it really does most of the time is point out what you call a problem and now many people will also look at it as a short fall in you,

When I was young I heard many of the older people of Italian heritage call all people who were not of Italian descent "the Americans". We would get angry and tell them we are all Americans, don't say that. I still hear other nationalities say "the Americans". I asked my father what was it like to be a very poor person of Italian descent when he was a young boy. He said the non-Italians would not pick up Italian kids walking home from school and that some of them would call them names. He said that was the past and that these same people are now his friends. He also said if they didn't like him became of his nationality or religion it was their problem. My parents were always proud and patriotic Americans. He didn't use these people as an excuse not to succeed. He never used the "if" word. He went on to become a wealthy person.

My mother was a short and very heavy person. She was very poor as a child, but she didn't dwell on the fact of how poor she had been. She would rather tell us about the fun things she did when she was young. Her children and grand children adored her. Mom had very fat arms. As a child I would wiggle the fat and laugh. Mom got a kick out of me doing this. Many years later my daughter would do the same thing and mom would laugh with her. She knew this was all part of our love for her. The grandchildren thought this person with a fifth grade education was the smartest person in the world. When it came to life and it's problems. If they needed advice they liked to go to grand mom and get her opinion, They thought grand mom really understood them and their problems. Mom didn't use the "if"word,

Move on with your life. Your future can't be written, it is only what you make it. If money can replace it, don't worry about it. Remember De Marco's Law. Recover and make this a positive experience.

twenty-four

EPILOGUE

*L*ife is how you interpret it

You must always remember De Marco's law it's not the amount of mistakes or the size of the mistake that counts. What counts is how well you recover. PRESS ON...

If you remember De Marco's law you will be an optimist and not a pessimist. When things go wrong the optimist will see it as a learning experience. You are having a wedding reception in a tent. The tent collapsed during a storm. The optimist will tell this story many times and laugh about the experience. The pessimist will continue to tell people how this incident ruined their wedding reception.

Life is how you see it. A young soldier on a beach in Hawaii writes home to his mother that he is telling his friend about how he can't wait to get home and eat some of his mother's spaghetti. The mother is very excited that he is thinking about her and she can't wait to cook that meal for him. All things and people are how you see them. Your home, your car, your past are all in your mind. You must be positive.

You have to believe in yourself and remember every day on earth is a magic time. Don't let time become your enemy.

We must be creative and be able to do things different then others. There are many positive ways you can be different. Does a teacher always have to sit behind a desk? How about sometimes sitting on the desk? Don't be obsessed with fact – learn how to think. The so called fact might actually be wrong. You can make some people believe if you eat a rabbit it will make you run faster. Our enemies are mainly in ourselves.

Your introduction is the most important part of an interview or when you meet someone. A profound amount is occurring non verbally. People are generating impressions of others and judging others skills and traits within only a few seconds.

We must know how to think not just what to think. Are all those foods they build up really taste that good or is it mainly in our heads? Are we really going to run out of energy or are we going to find new sources such as hydrogen, sun, wind and many other sources? Remember if you put all your eggs in one basket you better keep an eye on that basket. The most important friend should be inside your-self. You must always leave the cage door open so that the bird can return.

Do we always have to follow the crowd? Does a speech or book really have to be a minimum length. Lincoln's Gettysburg Address was only 272 words and only took two minutes. Lincoln not only was a great president but he also had a sense of humor and loved to tell jokes. He said, "a woman said he was the ugliest man in the world." He said, "I can't help it." She said, "you could have stayed home." When elected to congress he filled out the square "what is your education?" He wrote in defective.

We will always have problems but we must also always learn from our past mistakes, recover and PRESS ON.... After a storm things get greener. This is also true in our lives. It is much better if you make love with your mind and hands instead of your eyes.

Don't jump off a cliff when the tide is out. Remember everything begins in the brain. Always send your life in a positive direction. **There is a saying "angels can fly because they take themselves lightly.**

Don't waste your life. Learn how to reason and think. Many people have partners that snore very loud. Instead of complaining think of the snoring as a beautiful lullaby, actually think of it as a sleep medication.

Spend more time enjoying a wide variety of people. Blind people can over hear a lot because many people think they also can't hear. I see said the blind man. I hear a liar said the deaf man. It is much more enjoyable to have a wide variety of friends. A shortage of love is much more important than a shortage of material things.

Times will continue to change and we must be prepared for these changes. Airlines use to have large cabin crews. They say in the future there will only be a captain and a dog in the cockpit. The captain is there to tell the passengers this your captain speaking and to feed the dog. The dog will be there to bite the captain if the captains tries to touch the controls.

There is nothing worse then living a boring life. It is much better to say "I don't know where

I'm going, but I'm on my way? Jimmy Durante always said, "you ain't seen nothing yet." That is true in all our lives, we really don't know what the future will bring. It will be much more enjoyable if we learn from our past instead of brewing over our past. At the end of a storm is a golden sky. This is also true in our lives, if we learn that we must always recover and walk on with hope in our hearts. Popeye said, "I'm strong to the finish because I eat my spinach." We must make our lives fit each situation and fashion our tomorrows from mistakes of yesterday. Remember the rabbit had the speed but the turtle won the race. Don't be like the mouse going around and around on a wheel, **or a person who not only can't see the forest because of the trees, but they even have to count each leaf on the tree. The best way to apply De Marco's Law is be <u>positive</u>. Your home and everything else is how you see it. If you are camping in a tent you should see all the land around you as part of your home.**

Keep humor in your life. Two people at a dull party; one said, "this is a very dull party I'm going to leave", the other one said, "that should help". Many people spend to much time at work. They must always say, I need

time to think
time to love
time to play

and time for you..

Remember De Marco's law and you will rise to the level of your expectations.

Thank You

There are those who are always especially nice

There are those who do favors without thinking twice

There are those who are thoughtful, helpful and kind

And you have always been all of these things combined.

Thank you so much.

We must all try to be this kind of person. Many people can use our kindness and help. This kind and helpful person will be paid back many times over. The greatest payback you can receive is the great satisfaction you get by being positive and giving to others.

PRESS ON...

ABOUT THE AUTHOR

Louis De Marco is a retired Air Force navigator. He has traveled and lived in many parts of the world.

He has an undergraduate degree from the University of Nebraska. A masters in political science from the University of Arkansas and a master in counseling from Ball State University.

He worked as a social action officer in the US Air Force counseling Air Force personnel in drug, alcohol and other area's.

After retirement he served as the mayor of Hammonton, New Jersey and taught psychology and sociology at Atlantic Community College, New Jersey

Printed in the United States
2474